MAYER SMITH

The Fortune She Didn't Want

Copyright © 2025 by Mayer Smith

All rights reserved. No part of this publication may be reproduced, stored or transmitted in any form or by any means, electronic, mechanical, photocopying, recording, scanning, or otherwise without written permission from the publisher. It is illegal to copy this book, post it to a website, or distribute it by any other means without permission.

This novel is entirely a work of fiction. The names, characters and incidents portrayed in it are the work of the author's imagination. Any resemblance to actual persons, living or dead, events or localities is entirely coincidental.

Mayer Smith asserts the moral right to be identified as the author of this work.

Mayer Smith has no responsibility for the persistence or accuracy of URLs for external or third-party Internet Websites referred to in this publication and does not guarantee that any content on such Websites is, or will remain, accurate or appropriate.

Designations used by companies to distinguish their products are often claimed as trademarks. All brand names and product names used in this book and on its cover are trade names, service marks, trademarks and registered trademarks of their respective owners. The publishers and the book are not associated with any product or vendor mentioned in this book. None of the companies referenced within the book have endorsed the book.

First edition

*This book was professionally typeset on Reedsy.
Find out more at reedsy.com*

Contents

1	A Life of Luxury	1
2	Expectations	7
3	Encounter	14
4	Hidden Identity	21
5	The Unseen	27
6	Time and Space	34
7	Fragmented World	41
8	A Scientist's Obsession	48
9	Shadows	55
10	The Kiss	62
11	Fabric of Time	68
12	Unseen Connection	74
13	The Watchers	80
14	Falling Through Reality	86
15	Love Beyond Equations	93

One

A Life of Luxury

The grand chandelier above Elara cast its golden glow across the ballroom, refracting light onto the polished marble floors below. The scent of expensive perfume lingered in the air, mixing with the faint notes of classical music that echoed softly through the ornate space. Guests, draped in exquisite gowns and tailored suits, glided around her like ethereal beings—faces full of smiles that didn't quite reach their eyes, laughter that felt rehearsed, gestures measured and deliberate. Every inch of the room exuded wealth, status, and an unattainable perfection that Elara could never quite reconcile herself with.

She stood near the entrance, the weight of her surroundings pressing down on her chest like a thousand bricks. The room was an extravagant display of everything she didn't want. The gold-leafed frames, the towering floral arrangements, the extravagant crystal glasses—each piece was a reminder of the life she had been born into. A life of privilege that wasn't hers by choice, but by blood. She could almost taste the bitterness that had begun to settle in her mouth. It was the taste of her father's empire, of her mother's expectations, of the endless parade of parties and gatherings designed to showcase their family's wealth and power.

She adjusted the strap of her silver gown, the one she had been told to wear by her mother earlier that morning. It was a gown fit for royalty—elegant and refined, but it felt foreign on her body, like a costume that didn't belong. Every time she moved, it reminded her of the suffocating world she lived in. The life she had been groomed to embrace, but never truly wanted. Her heart longed for something else—a life filled with purpose, with meaning, with love that wasn't tied to social appearances and expectations.

Across the room, she could see her parents engaged in conversation with a group of influential businessmen and women. Her mother's laughter rang out, the sound so controlled and polished it seemed almost mechanical. Her father stood tall and imposing, his sharp eyes scanning the room with the calculated precision of a man who knew how to navigate every social situation to his advantage. Elara had always admired his intelligence, but never his lack of warmth. To him, people were either tools to be used or obstacles to be overcome. Love was a concept he seemed incapable of understanding, and it was a concept she herself had never seen in their grand house.

She pushed the thought away, forcing her gaze to wander over the crowd. The faces around her were all so familiar—people she had known her entire life, each of them wearing masks of their own. The laughter here was a mere formality, the conversations polite but shallow. No one truly cared about one another. They cared about what you could offer them, how you could help them climb higher in the social hierarchy. Elara's mind drifted to her upbringing, to the years of rehearsed smiles and hollow conversations she had endured. She had been taught to play the game from a young age, to smile and nod, to be the perfect daughter who made her family proud. But inside, she was empty, yearning for something more.

As the night stretched on, her thoughts wandered again, escaping the confines of the ballroom. She imagined herself somewhere else—anywhere else. A small cottage by the sea, the sound of waves crashing against the shore, the salty air filling her lungs. She could picture herself sitting on a porch, wearing simple clothes, holding a cup of tea in her hands. There, in that quiet place, she could be herself, without the weight of her family's legacy suffocating her every move.

"Elara, darling, you're not looking your best tonight," came the sharp voice of her mother, cutting through her reverie like a blade.

Elara's shoulders stiffened, and she turned to face her mother. She smiled faintly, masking the frustration that bubbled beneath her calm exterior. "I'm fine, Mother. Just a little tired, I suppose."

Her mother's eyes, cold and calculating, scanned her face.

"You're not pulling your weight in this little charade, are you?" she asked, her voice low, just enough for Elara to hear over the hum of the room.

Elara swallowed, keeping her expression neutral. "I'm doing what I can."

Her mother sighed dramatically, raising her hand to her forehead as if the burden of their family's reputation was too heavy to bear. "You need to do more than that. The Cunninghams are here tonight, and they're asking about you. You need to be more... presentable. Your father and I have big plans for you, Elara. You know that."

Elara's pulse quickened, the weight of her mother's words sinking into her chest. The Cunningham family. They were one of the wealthiest, most influential families in the city, and her mother had been pushing for a union between her and their son, Adrian Cunningham, for months. Adrian was handsome enough, tall and well-spoken, but Elara had never been interested in him. In fact, she found him as hollow as the world she was expected to fit into. Yet, her mother insisted that it was the perfect match—two powerful families coming together for mutual gain. It wasn't about love, and it never had been.

Her mother's sharp eyes studied her, waiting for a response. Elara knew better than to argue in front of everyone. She forced a smile, nodding. "I understand, Mother."

"Good," her mother said, her voice dripping with satisfaction.

"Now, go mingle. Make sure you're seen. You'll get the Cunninghams' attention, and your father and I will take care of the rest."

With that, her mother turned away, leaving Elara standing there, once again a puppet in a world she had no control over.

She pushed back the tears that threatened to surface, knowing better than to let anyone see her vulnerable. Taking a deep breath, she made her way toward the center of the room, where a group of guests were gathered around a grand display of champagne glasses. She tried to blend in, to take her place among the crowd, but as she glanced around, she felt more out of place than ever. She was invisible in plain sight, trapped by the wealth that surrounded her and the expectations that weighed her down.

And then, something caught her eye. A man. Standing by the large bay window, watching the night sky with a look of deep contemplation on his face. His presence was different from the others, not consumed by the superficialities that defined the party. There was a quiet intensity about him, a calmness that Elara couldn't help but be drawn to. His dark hair was slightly tousled, and his sharp jawline caught the light in a way that made him seem almost otherworldly.

For a moment, Elara simply watched him, transfixed by the stillness he exuded. She had never seen him before, and yet, there was something about him that felt familiar. Something that made her heart flutter, something that made her feel like she could finally breathe in a room that had always felt like a cage.

As though sensing her gaze, the man turned and looked directly at her. Their eyes met across the room, and for a brief moment, the world seemed to fade away. The clinking of glasses, the murmur of conversation, the laughter—everything disappeared. It was just her and him. A connection she couldn't explain, a pull she couldn't resist.

And just as quickly as it began, he looked away, disappearing into the crowd like a shadow. Elara stood frozen, her heart racing in her chest, her thoughts scattered.

She didn't know who he was, but she knew one thing for certain: tonight had just changed.

Two

Expectations

The evening after the gala felt strangely quiet, as if the world had turned in on itself, suffocating all the life and energy it had once held. Elara sat in her bedroom, the only sound the soft ticking of the clock on the wall, its rhythmic noise as unsettling as the weight that now pressed against her chest. Her mother's words from the night before replayed in her mind over and over again, each one landing with a heavy thud in her thoughts.

"You need to do more than that," her mother's voice echoed. "The Cunninghams are here tonight, and they're asking about you. You need to be more… presentable. Your father and I have big plans for you, Elara."

Elara rubbed her forehead with her fingers, her eyes shut tight, trying to block out the headache that had been building all evening. It wasn't the kind of headache that came from lack of sleep or tension, though. This was the kind of ache that grew from deep within—a feeling of entrapment, of helplessness. She knew her parents wanted her to marry Adrian Cunningham. They had been orchestrating this marriage since before she could remember. It was never about her happiness, never about love. It was about aligning two families, two fortunes, in the hopes of gaining more power, more influence.

Adrian Cunningham. His name tasted like ash in her mouth. He was a man of perfect appearances, the quintessential heir to a fortune, polished and well-mannered. But he was nothing like the man who had caught her eye last night—the stranger with the quiet intensity, the one who had stood by the bay window. She had only seen him for a fleeting moment, but that moment had burned into her mind, like a whisper she couldn't shake.

But the stranger was just that—a stranger. And he was no part of her world. There was no place for people like him in the carefully curated existence she was expected to lead. Her heart fluttered with an aching longing that she didn't know how to extinguish. She had never been given the freedom to follow her heart, to pursue love without the weight of obligation and expectation. Her parents had laid out her entire life for her, from her future husband to the way she would carry herself in public, to the very way she should dress.

Elara stood up from her chair and walked to the window, her eyes automatically seeking out the sprawling city skyline. The lights flickered in the distance like a thousand stars, each one a small beacon of hope. It was a view she had grown accustomed to, but tonight, it felt far away, unreachable. The city seemed like a reflection of her life—beautiful, polished, and cold. She closed her eyes, and in her mind's eye, she could see herself walking away from all of it—down into the city streets, free from her parents' reach, free from the shackles of a life that had never been her own.

But she knew better than to entertain such thoughts. She couldn't leave. Not yet, anyway. Her family would never allow it. The strings that held her were invisible, but they were strong enough to keep her firmly tethered in this gilded cage. She had learned that lesson long ago—there was no running away. Not without consequences.

Her phone buzzed on the desk beside her, jolting her from her thoughts. She glanced down at the screen, knowing without checking that it was her mother. Elara hesitated for a moment before answering.

"Hello, Mother," she said, trying to keep her voice steady.

"Elara, darling," her mother's voice was tight with authority. "I need you to come to the family office tomorrow. We need to discuss some details about the Cunninghams' visit next week."

Elara felt her heart sink, her throat constricting. The visit. Adrian. Everything about it made her want to curl up and disappear. She had no interest in discussing wedding plans with her mother, especially not with someone as distantly familiar as Adrian Cunningham.

"Of course," Elara said, her voice distant, even to her own ears. "I'll be there."

Her mother didn't say much more, as usual, but the conversation left Elara feeling hollow. She knew exactly what the meeting would entail—more pressure, more manipulation. Her parents would never let her breathe. Every decision she made would be weighed against their ambitions. Every choice she made would be scrutinized, dissected, and then molded into something that suited their purposes.

She set the phone down with a sigh and flopped back onto her bed, her mind racing. Was there any way out of this? Could she defy them? Could she walk away from the life that had been chosen for her and build one of her own? The thought filled her with both dread and a strange sense of excitement.

But then she thought of him. The man from last night. She didn't know his name, didn't know anything about him, but the way he had looked at her—so quietly, so intensely—made her feel as though, for the first time in her life, she had been seen for who she truly was. Not as Elara, the daughter of the wealthiest family in the city, but as Elara, the woman who longed for something real.

A knock at her door interrupted her thoughts, pulling her back into the present.

"Elara?" her father's voice called from the other side. "We need to talk."

Expectations

Her stomach turned at the sound of his voice. There was a coldness in it, a certain finality that always accompanied his conversations. Elara sat up quickly, smoothing out her gown, which still clung to her body like a second skin. She could hear the subtle command in his tone, and she knew that whatever conversation awaited her would be anything but pleasant.

"Come in," she called out, her voice soft.

The door creaked open, and her father entered, his tall frame casting a long shadow in the dimly lit room. He was dressed in a perfectly tailored suit, as always, his posture impeccable. His sharp eyes swept over her before he spoke.

"Elara, I've been meaning to talk to you about your future. About the future we've worked so hard to build," he said, his voice smooth but edged with something colder beneath.

She braced herself, knowing what was coming next. Her father had never been one for small talk. There was always an agenda. And tonight, it was no different.

"You've been spending far too much time daydreaming, haven't you?" he asked, his gaze narrowing. "Your mother and I have made our intentions clear. You will marry Adrian Cunningham. You will maintain the family legacy, as you were meant to."

Elara's heart stammered in her chest, the pressure mounting as her father's words hung in the air. Her throat tightened, but she said nothing. She couldn't argue. Not with him. Not with the man who had built an empire on his own and expected everyone around him to fall in line.

"You are the one who will carry our name forward, Elara. You cannot afford to be distracted by silly fantasies of romance," he continued, his voice growing colder with each word. "Adrian is perfect for you. His family is everything we need to solidify our standing in this city. You are not free to choose who you love. You are free to choose how you play your part."

Elara stood in silence, the weight of his words sinking in like a stone. Every ounce of her desire for freedom, for love, was being crushed under the weight of his expectations. She felt herself shrinking under his gaze, a helpless pawn in a game that wasn't of her making.

"I understand," she said quietly, though her heart screamed the opposite.

Her father gave her a sharp nod and turned to leave, but not before offering one last, chilling remark.

"You will not disappoint us, Elara. If you do, there will be consequences. Remember that."

The door clicked shut behind him, and Elara collapsed onto her bed, her hands trembling as she stared up at the ceiling. The room felt smaller now, the walls closing in on her. She had never felt more alone.

She closed her eyes, wishing for the impossible—for a life where she could be free to choose her own path. A life where love wasn't dictated by power, and where happiness wasn't just a mirage.

But all she had now was the weight of her family's expectations, and the flicker of a stranger's eyes that would forever haunt her heart.

Three

Encounter

The city had a way of stirring something inside Elara, a restlessness that she couldn't quite shake, no matter how much her family's wealth smothered the life out of her. She'd always been told that the bright lights of the city represented success, that each gleaming skyscraper was a symbol of the power her family had cultivated over decades. But as she stood on the balcony of her family's penthouse suite, looking down at the labyrinth of streets below, she couldn't shake the feeling that it was all just an illusion. A glittering cage. A façade designed to hide the emptiness that lay beneath.

Elara sighed, leaning her elbows against the cold metal of the balcony railing, the wind whipping her long hair around her face. The city was alive tonight, the streets pulsating with the energy of a thousand people who, like her, were chasing something they couldn't quite define. She longed to be part of it, to be one of the nameless faces drifting through the crowd, free from the expectations that always loomed over her.

Her mother's voice echoed in her mind, the words she had said earlier that day. "You're running out of time, Elara. Adrian is waiting for you to make up your mind." It felt as though the world around her was pressing in on her, suffocating her with its demands. She hated how easily her life had been mapped out for her, every step taken to ensure that her family's wealth and legacy would be preserved. But what about her? What about the dreams she had hidden deep within herself, the ones that were never allowed to see the light of day?

With a final, heavy sigh, Elara stepped back from the railing, glancing at the ornate clock on the wall. It was late, but she couldn't stay cooped up in the penthouse any longer. She needed to get away, even if just for a few hours. For once, she wanted to escape the suffocating world of wealth and expectations and breathe in something real.

Without thinking, she grabbed her coat and slipped out the door, making her way down to the parking garage. Her personal driver was always available, but tonight, she needed to be alone. She needed to lose herself in the anonymity of the city, where no one would recognize her as the daughter of the wealthy Van Wynt family.

She drove herself, her fingers gripping the steering wheel tightly as she navigated through the city streets. The car hummed beneath her, a reminder of the life she had been given. But for tonight, it didn't matter. Tonight, she wasn't Elara Van Wynt, the heiress. Tonight, she was just a woman trying to breathe.

The streets were bustling, full of life. The bright lights of neon signs reflected off the wet pavement as she parked in a quiet side street and stepped out of the car. The air smelled faintly of rain, and the hum of the city was comforting in its constant motion. She walked down the street, her heels clicking against the concrete as she passed a series of small cafés, shops, and boutiques. Her eyes were drawn to the windows, where couples sat at tables, laughing and talking. It was all so normal, so real. Everything that she had longed for in the depths of her soul.

But then, as she turned the corner, something caught her eye. A small bookstore, tucked away between two buildings, its windows lined with shelves full of old books. The dim, golden glow of the lights inside created a sense of warmth, a stark contrast to the cold, sterile atmosphere of her home. It was the kind of place where you could lose yourself for hours, surrounded by stories and worlds that didn't care about who you were or what you had.

Without thinking, she walked inside.

The bell above the door chimed softly as she entered, and the smell of old paper and coffee enveloped her. It was small, with wooden bookshelves that reached up to the ceiling, filled with books that had stories to tell. The air was thick with the kind of quiet that made you feel as though you were entering a sanctuary. The soft murmur of voices from the few patrons in the store mingled with the faint sound of classical music playing in the background.

Encounter

Elara walked deeper into the store, her fingers trailing along the spines of the books as she passed by. For a moment, she lost herself in the rows of stories, each one a different world waiting to be discovered. She felt a sense of peace, a calmness that had eluded her for so long. Here, in this small, forgotten corner of the city, there were no expectations, no rules. There was only the quiet comfort of a bookshop, a place that promised escape.

As she moved towards the back of the store, something made her stop. A figure, seated at a small table near the window, caught her attention. He was bent over a notebook, his brow furrowed in concentration as he scribbled something down with a pencil. She couldn't see his face at first, but the posture, the way he leaned over the table so completely absorbed in whatever he was doing—it intrigued her.

Something about him seemed... different. He wasn't like the others in the store, the people who came in for a few minutes, picked out a book, and left. No, this man was here for something else. Something deeper. She watched him for a moment longer, her curiosity growing, before she realized she was staring and quickly turned her attention back to the books in front of her.

But then, as if sensing her gaze, the man looked up.

Their eyes met.

For a brief moment, Elara felt a jolt of recognition, something that startled her deep inside. It wasn't just the way he looked at her—there was something else in his eyes. A depth, a kind of understanding that no one had ever offered her before. His gaze wasn't filled with the usual pretense or expectation. It was simply... real.

The moment stretched, time slowing as they held each other's gaze across the room. She felt a flutter in her chest, a strange sensation that she couldn't name. It was as though everything in the world had narrowed down to this one moment, this one connection.

The man's lips quirked into a small, knowing smile, as if he recognized something in her too. His gaze softened, and he stood slowly, pushing his chair back with a gentle scrape.

Elara hesitated, unsure of what to do. She wasn't accustomed to being approached like this. Men didn't usually look at her like this—not with curiosity, not with understanding. They looked at her for what she could provide, for her family's wealth, for the status she represented. But this man... he saw her.

He took a step toward her, and the soft sound of his shoes against the wooden floor was the only noise that filled the room. The tension in the air was palpable, like the anticipation before a storm.

"Forgive me," he said, his voice low, smooth, and undeniably warm. "I didn't mean to stare. But you seem... different. Not like the people I usually see around here."

Elara blinked, thrown off balance by his words. For a moment, she couldn't speak, her mind racing to find the right response. But his presence, his calm, steady gaze, made it feel like she had all the time in the world.

"I… I was just looking at the books," she said finally, her voice a little softer than she intended. "This is a lovely bookstore."

He nodded, his smile deepening slightly. "Yes, it's one of my favorite places. There's something about the silence here, don't you think?"

Elara smiled, feeling an unfamiliar warmth bloom in her chest. "Yes. It's… peaceful."

For a moment, they simply stood there, the words lingering between them. Then, almost as if on instinct, the man extended his hand.

"My name is Julian," he said, his voice carrying a hint of amusement. "And you are?"

Elara hesitated. She didn't give her name to strangers. Especially not in a place like this. But there was something about Julian, something in the way he looked at her, that made her want to be honest for the first time in a long while.

"Elara," she said, offering him a small smile. "Elara Van Wynt."

He raised an eyebrow, his interest piqued. "Van Wynt? That's quite the name."

She stiffened, but he didn't seem to notice. "It's just a name," she replied quietly. "It's not as important as you might think."

Julian studied her for a moment, his gaze unwavering. "Maybe," he said thoughtfully. "But it's not every day that I meet someone who doesn't seem to care about their name."

Elara felt a strange pull towards him, an instinct that told her she needed to know more about him. And for the first time in what felt like forever, she didn't feel like an heiress with a legacy to uphold. She just felt… human.

"I'm glad we met, Elara," Julian said, his smile genuine. "And I hope we meet again."

With that, he turned and walked toward the door, leaving Elara standing there, her heart racing in her chest.

She didn't know it yet, but this chance encounter was the beginning of something that would change everything.

Four

Hidden Identity

―――

Elara sat on the edge of her bed, her fingers absentmindedly tracing the rim of her coffee cup. The warmth of the drink did little to soothe the unsettling feeling that had settled in her stomach. The events of the night before played over and over in her mind like a film reel, each frame more vivid than the last. She hadn't expected to meet someone like Julian. The encounter, so sudden and so unexpected, had turned her world on its head in the space of a few minutes. She had spent the entire evening reflecting on it, turning over every word they had exchanged, every glance they had shared.

For the first time in years, Elara felt alive. For the first time in a long while, she felt seen. Not as the daughter of the Van Wynt family, not as the heiress with a fortune to protect, but as a woman—just a woman—who could exist outside the confines of her gilded cage.

But it was also dangerous.

Her fingers tightened around the cup, and she set it down with a soft clink. The sense of guilt that always followed moments of unguarded joy crept in, reminding her of her reality. There were boundaries she could not cross, no matter how badly she wanted to. She couldn't afford to let herself get attached to someone like Julian. The world she had been born into didn't allow for it. She had no room for the simple, fleeting pleasures of a normal life. Her life had been charted for her from the very beginning, and as much as she might wish otherwise, she had no choice but to follow the path laid out for her.

Her phone buzzed on the bedside table, cutting through the silence. Elara glanced at the screen and immediately felt her stomach twist.

It was her mother.

She took a deep breath before answering. "Hello, Mother."

"Elara," came her mother's cold voice on the other end. "I need you to come home immediately. Your father and I have made arrangements for you. Adrian will be over this evening to discuss the details of the engagement. You're to make yourself available."

Elara's pulse quickened at the mention of Adrian's name. The very thought of him made her skin crawl. She had always felt that he was the perfect match for her in the way that a business merger could be perfect—unemotional, calculated, and mutually beneficial. But it was never love. It wasn't even close.

"I'll be there," she said softly, her voice betraying none of the frustration that churned within her.

"Good," her mother responded. "Be sure you're presentable. Adrian will expect nothing less."

The call ended abruptly, and Elara stared at the phone for a moment, trying to shake the unease that had settled in her chest. Her mother's words echoed in her mind, like a constant reminder of everything she was expected to be. She had no choice but to attend this meeting, to put on the façade and pretend that this was what she wanted. But somewhere deep inside her, a part of her rebelled. The part of her that longed for something real, something untouched by the expectations of wealth and power.

She couldn't deny the pull she felt towards Julian. There was a connection there—something she hadn't experienced in years. It terrified her. Because she knew the consequences of allowing herself to feel anything for him. He was someone outside her world, someone who didn't know who she was or what she represented. But that was precisely what made him so dangerous. His lack of knowledge was the very thing that drew her in. He didn't care about her family's name or the wealth that came with it. He saw her. He truly saw her, for who she was, not what she had.

But she couldn't let herself get too close. She couldn't risk it.

The Fortune She Didn't Want

The life she was born into would never allow it.

Later that evening, Elara stood in front of the full-length mirror in her bedroom, staring at her reflection. Her hair was carefully styled, her makeup flawless, and she wore a dress that was meant to exude elegance and grace. The dress was a deep navy blue, simple but luxurious, hugging her body in a way that felt more like a second skin than a piece of clothing. She looked the part of the perfect daughter, the poised and polished woman that the world expected her to be.

But underneath the surface, Elara felt anything but perfect. She felt like a stranger in her own skin. Every time she looked in the mirror, she saw the woman who was trapped by expectations, by her family's relentless pursuit of power and status. The woman in the mirror wasn't her. Not really. She was a construct, a carefully crafted image meant to impress and to conform.

The sound of the doorbell rang through the house, jolting her from her thoughts. She took a deep breath, straightening her back, and walked toward the door. As she reached for the handle, her mind flashed to Julian. The memory of his smile, of the way he had looked at her with those intense, searching eyes, made her heart race. She quickly pushed the thought aside and opened the door.

Adrian Cunningham stood on the doorstep, looking every bit the part of the perfect fiancé. Tall, impeccably dressed, with a smile that was just charming enough to pass for genuine but not quite warm enough to be real. He greeted her with a firm handshake, his grip cold and controlled, just like everything about him.

"Good evening, Elara," Adrian said, his voice smooth and polished. "I trust you're well?"

"I'm fine," Elara replied, her voice steady, though her heart wasn't in it. "Please, come in."

As Adrian stepped inside, she could feel the weight of his gaze on her, as if he was inspecting her every move, every detail. She felt like an object, something to be appraised, something to be carefully studied and found wanting. She had never been able to shake the feeling when she was around him.

They made their way to the sitting room, where her parents were already waiting. Elara took her seat, forcing a smile as Adrian sat down beside her, his presence suffocating in its perfection. They exchanged pleasantries, the conversation polite but devoid of warmth. As always, the talk turned to their future, to the plans that had already been made for them. Their wedding, the merging of two powerful families, the legacy they would create together.

Elara felt herself slipping away as the conversation continued. It was all so calculated, so orchestrated. She was nothing more than a pawn in this game, a piece to be moved when necessary. She tried to focus on the words, but her thoughts kept drifting back to Julian. What was he doing right now? Was he thinking about her? Did he wonder if she would come back to the bookstore again?

"Elara?" her father's voice cut through her thoughts, snapping her back to reality. "Are you listening?"

She blinked, meeting her father's gaze. His expression was stern, waiting for her response. The weight of his stare was enough to make her stomach churn.

"Yes, Father," she said, forcing herself to smile. "I'm listening."

Adrian leaned in slightly, his eyes narrowing ever so slightly as he studied her. "Good," he said, his voice just a bit too smooth. "We were discussing the details of our engagement. The wedding is soon, and we'll need to begin preparations. Your family's presence is of utmost importance. You understand that, don't you?"

Elara nodded, but her mind was elsewhere. The words seemed to echo hollowly in her ears, a reminder that her life wasn't hers to control. Her entire future had already been mapped out for her, and there was nothing she could do to change it.

But then, just as quickly as the thought arrived, another one took its place. The thought of Julian. The thought of being free. The thought of escaping this suffocating world and stepping into something unknown, something real.

It was a dangerous thought. And she knew it.

But it was the only thought that made her feel alive.

Five

The Unseen

Elara sat at the dinner table, her fingers absentmindedly swirling the wine in her glass. The rich red liquid caught the candlelight, casting a warm glow across the room, but it did little to soften the chill that had settled in her chest. The evening had been a blur of forced smiles, polite conversation, and a steady stream of small talk with Adrian. Every word that left his lips seemed rehearsed, calculated, designed to further solidify the union between their families. She had been trained her entire life to navigate these kinds of dinners, to act as though she was interested in every detail of the conversation, when all she wanted was to escape.

Her father sat across from her, his eyes flicking between the two of them as if he were monitoring the interaction. Her mother was at the far end of the table, her sharp gaze never leaving Elara for too long. She could almost feel the weight of their expectations pressing down on her, suffocating her with every moment.

She took a sip of her wine, the liquid bitter on her tongue, and tried to focus on the conversation in front of her. Adrian was talking about his latest business venture—another luxury development project in the city, designed to further expand the Cunningham family's influence. He spoke with a self-assurance that bordered on arrogance, as though the world was just waiting for him to make the next move. Elara barely heard the words, her thoughts drifting back to the bookstore.

The memory of Julian lingered in her mind like a shadow she couldn't shake. The way he had looked at her with those knowing eyes, the way his presence had felt so real, so grounded. It was a stark contrast to the polished, cold façade that Adrian presented. Julian hadn't asked her about her family's fortune, hadn't mentioned the business empire that her father had built from the ground up. He hadn't cared about any of that. He had seen her, just as she was, and for the first time in ages, Elara had felt like she was more than just a product of her name.

She could feel her pulse quickening as she thought about him again. He had been a stranger, but something about their brief encounter had left an impression that she couldn't ignore. What had he seen in her? What was it that had drawn him to her in the first place? She couldn't stop thinking about it—the quiet intensity in his eyes, the way he seemed to understand her without a single word being spoken.

"Elara," Adrian's voice broke through her thoughts, pulling her back to the present. His tone was laced with impatience, and she could tell he wasn't used to being ignored. "Are you listening?"

She blinked, forcing her attention back to him. "Yes, of course," she said quickly, offering a smile that didn't quite reach her eyes.

"You seem distracted," Adrian said, his eyes narrowing slightly. "Something on your mind?"

Elara felt the pressure of his gaze, and her stomach twisted. She knew he was trying to read her, trying to figure out what was wrong. But how could she explain? How could she tell him that her thoughts were consumed with a man she barely knew, a man who was nothing like him, a man who made her feel something real?

"I'm just… tired," she said, offering a weak excuse.

Adrian didn't seem convinced, but he didn't press the issue further. Instead, he picked up his glass of wine and took a long sip, his gaze flicking toward her father. The conversation shifted again, this time turning to their upcoming wedding plans. Elara felt her chest tighten as her father began discussing the details with Adrian, outlining the arrangements for the grand event. Every word felt like a weight pressing down on her, each decision made without her consent. Her life, her future, being planned for her by people who had no interest in her happiness—only in their own desires.

She could feel the walls of the room closing in, the air growing heavier with each passing moment. She needed to leave. She needed to get away from all of this, even if it was just for a few minutes, to breathe, to think clearly.

"Excuse me," Elara said abruptly, pushing her chair back from the table. Her voice trembled slightly, betraying the turmoil she was feeling inside. "I need some air."

Before either Adrian or her father could respond, she stood and walked quickly out of the room, her heels clicking sharply on the marble floors. She didn't look back. She couldn't bear to see the expressions on their faces, the disapproval that she knew would be written there.

She made her way to the front door, stepping out into the cool night air. The sky was clear, and the stars glittered above, a reminder of the vastness of the world beyond her family's towering estate. She took a deep breath, trying to steady herself, to calm the storm of emotions that raged inside her. But nothing seemed to help. The ache in her chest, the feeling of being trapped, only grew stronger.

"Elara."

The voice came from behind her, and she froze. She didn't need to turn around to know who it was. Adrian's voice was smooth, yet there was an edge to it now, a sharpness that hadn't been there before. She could hear the click of his footsteps behind her as he approached, his presence oppressive, just as it had been at dinner.

The Unseen

"You're running away again," he said, his tone colder now, more controlled. "Is this how you plan on handling things? By avoiding them?"

Elara's heart raced in her chest as she forced herself to face him. Adrian was standing a few feet away, his jaw tight, his eyes searching her face. He was angry now, and there was a certain finality in his stance, as if he had decided she was a problem to be solved. She could feel the pressure mounting, the expectations weighing on her, but she refused to let him see how much he affected her.

"I just needed some space," she said, her voice steady, though the words felt like a lie. She could feel the anger building inside her, the frustration of being treated like an object, a means to an end. "I'm not a child, Adrian. I don't need to be handled like one."

He took a step closer, his eyes narrowing. "I'm not treating you like a child, Elara. But I won't stand for this behavior. We're supposed to be partners in this, and yet you're constantly pulling away. Do you really think this is the way to make a marriage work?"

She opened her mouth to respond, but before she could, the sound of a car engine cut through the air, distant at first, then growing louder as it approached. Elara's heart skipped a beat. For a fleeting moment, she thought she might be imagining it, but then, she heard it again—the unmistakable sound of a car pulling into the driveway.

It wasn't Adrian's car. And it wasn't one of the household vehicles.

Without thinking, Elara turned toward the street, her gaze darting in the direction of the sound. And there, at the end of the driveway, a dark sedan came into view. Her breath caught in her throat as she recognized the figure behind the wheel.

It was Julian.

Her pulse quickened as the car rolled to a stop, the engine shutting off with a soft click. Elara stood frozen, staring at the vehicle as the door opened and Julian stepped out. His presence, calm and assured, seemed to cut through the tension in the air, his very being an anchor to a world she desperately longed to be a part of. He glanced toward her, his gaze meeting hers across the distance, and for a moment, the world seemed to stand still.

But then, as quickly as the connection had been made, it snapped. Adrian's voice broke through the moment, his words filled with ice. "Who is that?"

Elara's heart sank. She turned slowly back to face him, her breath unsteady in her chest. "It's no one," she said quickly, her voice tight. "Just someone I met... recently."

Adrian's eyes darkened, his expression hardening. He could sense it—the shift in her, the change in the air. But before he could say anything else, Julian took a step forward, his gaze never leaving Elara's.

The Unseen

The tension between the three of them was thick, suffocating, and for the first time, Elara realized that her carefully constructed world had begun to unravel. She didn't know what would happen next. She didn't know what this meant for her future, for the choices she had made, but one thing was clear: she could no longer pretend that she didn't feel the pull between her and Julian.

And she could no longer pretend that the life she was being forced into was the one she truly wanted.

The unseen connection between her and Julian was far stronger than she could have ever anticipated, and it was beginning to pull her in a direction she wasn't ready to face.

Six

Time and Space

The evening had fallen into a tense silence after Julian's arrival. Elara could feel the weight of Adrian's gaze burning into her back as she stood in the driveway, torn between the world she knew and the one she had barely dared to imagine. Adrian had said nothing further as he stood there, his expression a mixture of confusion and barely concealed frustration. It seemed as though time had paused, every moment dragging on like a slow-motion scene from a movie, too surreal to fully grasp.

Julian had taken his time approaching her, his calm demeanor not wavering as he walked toward her in measured steps. The distance between them felt like an eternity, as if the universe was holding its breath, waiting for something to unfold.

"Elara," Julian's voice was soft, cutting through the charged silence like a knife, the sound so familiar already that it made her chest tighten. His gaze met hers, steady, unwavering. In his eyes, there was no judgment, no pretense—only an invitation to something she could not name, something that had been slowly building in her heart since their first meeting. "Are you okay?"

She opened her mouth to answer, but the words caught in her throat. What could she say? That she was fine? That she wasn't being suffocated by the life she had been forced into? That she wasn't drowning in the expectations of her family and the world they had built around her? No. She couldn't say that. She wasn't fine. She hadn't been fine for a long time.

"I… I didn't expect you," she said, her voice trembling slightly. She forced herself to look away from him, glancing back at Adrian. He hadn't moved, still standing in the same place, his expression hardening with every passing second. The situation had become far more complicated than Elara could have imagined.

"I know," Julian said, his voice low but comforting. "But I couldn't stay away. I had to see you again."

Her heart skipped a beat at the words, the honesty in them taking her by surprise. It was so rare for anyone, especially men in her world, to be so open, so unguarded. And that was what made Julian different. He wasn't playing the game, wasn't pretending to be someone he wasn't. He wasn't here for her family's wealth or the status that came with her name. He was here for her.

A deep, unsettling sense of guilt twisted inside her at the thought. She could feel Adrian's eyes on her like a physical presence, burning a hole in her back. He was watching her, waiting for her to say something, to explain herself. But Elara didn't have the answers. She didn't even know what she wanted anymore.

She turned slowly to face Adrian, trying to muster the courage to speak. "Adrian, this is… Julian," she said, her voice faltering as she gestured toward him. The words felt wrong, out of place. This wasn't how it was supposed to be. But she couldn't ignore the fact that Julian had come to her, that his presence had completely shifted the balance of everything. It was too late to pretend.

Adrian's eyes flicked from her to Julian, his lips curling into a tight smile that never reached his eyes. "Julian, I presume?" His voice dripped with politeness, but Elara could hear the underlying edge. "You're… a friend of Elara's?"

Julian's expression remained impassive, unaffected by Adrian's coldness. "Yes," he said, his gaze flicking briefly to Elara before locking back onto Adrian. "We met recently. I just wanted to make sure she was all right."

There was a brief, tense silence. Adrian didn't respond immediately, instead taking a slow step forward. Elara could feel the tension between the two men building, a subtle but undeniable power struggle. She hated the feeling—the feeling of being pulled between two worlds, two expectations. She had no idea how to navigate it, how to keep herself from falling apart in the process.

"Is that so?" Adrian said, his voice colder now. He was staring at Julian with a look of mild amusement, but it was the kind of amusement that made Elara's stomach turn. It was the look of a man who was trying to gain control of a situation he didn't fully understand.

"I think it's time for you to leave," Adrian continued, his voice sharper now. "This is a private matter, and I don't appreciate unexpected visitors."

Julian didn't flinch. He didn't back down. He simply nodded, his eyes never leaving Adrian's. "Of course," he said, his tone calm. "But I'll leave on one condition."

Adrian raised an eyebrow, clearly intrigued. Elara could see the tension in his posture, the way his body stiffened in preparation for whatever challenge Julian was about to throw at him. She could sense the bubbling frustration inside Adrian, could feel the way he was trying to regain control of the situation. But Julian didn't seem intimidated. He wasn't like everyone else who had ever walked into this world. He wasn't here to be manipulated.

"You'll leave," Julian said, his voice quiet but firm, "if Elara asks you to."

The words hit Elara like a thunderclap, reverberating through her entire being. She felt the weight of them in her chest, in her stomach. A part of her wanted to run, to shrink back, to take back everything she had allowed herself to feel. But another part—the part that had been yearning for something real, something beyond the suffocating constraints of her life—felt a flicker of hope.

She turned slowly to face Julian, her heart racing in her chest. The words she had been holding back for so long felt like they were finally breaking free, bubbling to the surface. She wasn't ready to make a decision, but for the first time in a long while, she didn't want to hide. She didn't want to pretend.

Adrian's eyes flicked from her to Julian, his face hardening with anger. The smile had disappeared completely, replaced by a look of cold determination. He could feel the shift too. He knew what was happening, what this meant.

"Elara," Adrian's voice was low now, dangerously soft. "You can't be serious."

She swallowed hard, the weight of the decision pressing down on her. She couldn't go back. She couldn't unsee what Julian had shown her—the possibility of something real.

"Julian," Elara said softly, her voice barely above a whisper. "Please... stay."

The words left her mouth before she could fully process them, and for a moment, it felt like time itself had stopped. Adrian's face went white with fury, his eyes wide with disbelief. Julian's expression softened, and though he didn't say anything, Elara could see the relief in his eyes.

Adrian, however, was another story.

"You don't understand, Elara," Adrian said through clenched teeth. "You think this is some kind of game? You think you can just… throw it all away for a… for a stranger?"

His words cut through her like a blade. She could feel the guilt rising, the fear of the unknown pulling at her, but it wasn't enough to erase the truth she had just spoken. For the first time, Elara realized that her heart wasn't in the life she was supposed to lead. She wasn't living for her family, for the expectations they placed on her. She was living for something else, something that had been buried deep inside her for far too long.

"This isn't a game, Adrian," Elara said, her voice stronger now. "This is my life."

With that, she turned to Julian, meeting his gaze with a newfound sense of clarity. "I want to see where this goes," she said, her voice steady. "I don't know what will happen. But I'm not going back to a life of pretending. Not anymore."

Julian stepped forward, his hand reaching out toward her. Elara took it without hesitation, feeling the warmth of his touch, the grounding presence that had been missing from her life for far too long. She knew there were no easy answers, no guarantees. But for the first time in what felt like forever, she was choosing something that was real.

Adrian's eyes narrowed, his face a mask of anger and disbelief.

"You've made your choice, then," he said, his voice cold and final.

Elara didn't answer. She didn't need to. She knew what she had chosen. And for the first time in her life, that was enough.

As she walked away from Adrian and toward Julian, Elara felt something shift inside her. The past was behind her, and the future was still uncertain. But for the first time, she wasn't afraid to face it.

She was free. And nothing would ever be the same again.

Seven

Fragmented World

The days that followed were a blur of confusion, exhilaration, and deep introspection. Elara had stepped into uncharted territory, her once controlled existence now disrupted by a choice that felt both freeing and terrifying. Adrian's departure had been swift, his angry words lingering in the air long after he had stormed off. Her parents, unsurprisingly, had been less than pleased with her defiance, but they hadn't yet fully realized the gravity of her decision. They continued with their calculated conversations, as if the world hadn't shifted beneath their feet, but Elara could feel it in every word, every glance exchanged between her father and mother.

She hadn't been prepared for the aftermath. She hadn't known what it would feel like to break free from the expectations, to carve out her own path. But now, as she stood in the quiet of her room, staring at the reflection in the mirror, she realized she was no longer the woman she had once been. She was no longer simply Elara Van Wynt, the heiress destined to fulfill her family's plans. She was someone else, someone unknown, and the uncertainty of it all left her feeling both liberated and vulnerable.

The evening after Adrian's abrupt departure, she found herself alone in her private study, the room lined with bookshelves and soft light from the desk lamp illuminating her face. She had been avoiding her phone, ignoring the texts and calls from her mother. But she knew she couldn't keep running from her reality forever. She had made her decision—now she had to figure out how to live with it.

As she stared at the empty space where her reflection had once been a symbol of who she was, a knock at the door interrupted her thoughts.

"Elara?"

The voice that came from the other side of the door was Julian's, and just hearing it made her heart race. She had been thinking about him constantly since their last meeting. His presence felt like an anchor, like a connection to something real in a world that seemed increasingly fragmented. She had never known a person like him—someone who didn't care about wealth, about status, about the masks people wore. Julian saw her, truly saw her, in a way no one else ever had.

"Elara?" His voice was soft but insistent, a sound that made her want to hide and yet made her want to open the door all at once.

She stood up from the chair, moving toward the door with hesitant steps. Her breath caught in her throat as she reached for the handle, opening it to reveal him standing on the other side. His dark eyes were filled with warmth, yet there was a trace of concern in them, as if he were waiting for her to say something—anything—that would explain the silence between them since that night.

"Julian," she said, her voice quiet, almost unsure. She hadn't known what to expect when she opened the door. The uncertainty was thick between them, and she wasn't sure where they stood, where she stood in relation to him.

"May I come in?" he asked, his voice gentle, yet carrying the weight of something deeper. Elara stepped aside without a word, and Julian walked in, his presence filling the room like the calm after a storm.

He didn't sit right away. Instead, he walked over to the window, looking out at the city lights stretching endlessly into the night. The faint hum of traffic, the distant sound of voices—it was a strange sort of music to Elara, a symphony of lives being lived outside the confines of her mansion. The world outside was chaotic, unpredictable, and free. And in that moment, it felt like the place where she belonged.

"I didn't know if you wanted me here," Julian said after a long pause, his back still turned to her. "I didn't want to intrude."

Elara stood silently for a moment, taking in the depth of his words. He was right. She hadn't known what to expect from him after everything that had happened. She had expected him to disappear, to walk away from the mess she had made of her life. But here he was, standing in front of her, waiting for her to respond. His presence was both a comfort and a reminder that the life she had known before was slipping further away.

"I want you here," she said, her voice stronger than she had expected it to be. "I just... I didn't know what to say."

Julian turned then, his gaze meeting hers. The intensity in his eyes was enough to make her heart skip a beat, the connection between them undeniable. She had never felt more exposed, more vulnerable, and yet more certain of something in her life. It was as though the fractured pieces of her world had finally begun to come together, and it was Julian who was the missing piece she hadn't realized she was searching for.

"You don't have to say anything, Elara," Julian said, stepping closer to her. "I'm not here because I expect anything. I'm here because I want to be."

The words hung in the air between them, laden with unspoken promises. Elara's breath caught in her throat. Her mind raced, memories of her life flashing before her—her family's expectations, her engagement to Adrian, the life she had been born into. None of it mattered anymore. Nothing had ever felt as real as this moment, as Julian standing before her, offering her something she didn't fully understand but knew she needed.

She reached out without thinking, her hand finding his. The touch was electric, like a spark igniting between them. Julian's fingers tightened around hers, grounding her in the uncertainty of the moment. They stood there for a few moments, neither of them speaking, the silence stretching out around them like a cocoon. Elara could feel her heart pounding in her chest, the vulnerability of the situation making her second-guess herself. But as she looked into Julian's eyes, all of her fears seemed to dissipate.

"I don't know what I'm doing," Elara confessed, her voice shaking slightly. "I've spent my whole life pretending, trying to be what everyone wanted me to be. And now, I'm not sure where to go, who to turn to."

"You're not alone," Julian said softly, his thumb brushing over the back of her hand. "Not anymore. You don't have to pretend with me."

Elara felt a tear slip down her cheek before she could stop it. She hadn't realized how much she had needed to hear those words, how much she had longed for someone to tell her that it was okay to be herself. For so long, she had been locked in a cage of her own making, afraid to break free, afraid to be seen. But Julian... Julian made her feel like she wasn't just a reflection of her family's expectations. She was someone who deserved to be loved, to be free.

"Why are you doing this?" she whispered, her voice barely audible. "Why me?"

Julian smiled, a soft, genuine smile that made her heart ache. "Because I see you, Elara. And that's all that matters."

The simplicity of his words settled over her like a blanket, soothing the raw, jagged edges of her soul. She had never felt more exposed, more vulnerable, but at the same time, she had never felt more alive. She wasn't just the daughter of a powerful family, trapped in a life she didn't want. She was Elara. And for the first time, that was enough.

"I don't know what comes next," she said, her voice trembling. "But I know I want to find out. With you."

Julian's eyes softened as he gently cupped her face in his hands, wiping away the tear that had escaped her. "Then we'll find out together."

He leaned in, his lips brushing against her forehead in a tender, reassuring kiss. The world outside the window seemed to fade away, leaving only the two of them in this small, quiet moment of peace. It wasn't perfect. It wasn't the life she had been trained to live. But it was hers. And it was real.

For the first time in a long time, Elara felt like she had found a place where she truly belonged. In Julian's arms, she wasn't just someone's daughter, someone's future bride, someone's expectation. She was Elara, a woman with a choice, a woman with a future that was still hers to decide.

The world around them may have been fractured, broken in so many ways, but in that moment, Elara felt whole. And as she looked into Julian's eyes, she knew that no matter what the future held, this connection—this love—was the only thing that truly mattered.

Eight

A Scientist's Obsession

The world was falling away from Elara, piece by piece, every expectation, every plan, every carefully laid path she had followed since childhood crumbling to dust. She could feel it in her bones, the weight of it pressing against her chest, threatening to suffocate her. And yet, despite the suffocating pressure, there was something liberating about the unraveling of her life. Something that felt like freedom, like the possibility of something real, something untouched by the expectations that had defined her existence for so long.

As the days passed, she found herself pulled deeper into the world Julian had created—into a life that didn't demand perfection, that didn't demand her to be anyone other than who she truly was. With Julian, she didn't have to wear the mask. She didn't have to pretend. The connection between them had grown exponentially, each meeting, each shared moment of silence, deepening the bond that had been sparked between them.

But even in the midst of all this newness, Elara couldn't shake the anxiety that gnawed at her from the inside. She had chosen Julian. She had chosen a life of uncertainty, a life where love and freedom came with a price, but that choice was not without consequences. Her family was still out there, still waiting for her to come back, still demanding her compliance. The pressure was mounting, but Elara couldn't bring herself to regret her decision. Not yet.

The evening was thick with tension as Elara and Julian sat in his small, cluttered apartment. It was nothing like the opulence of her family's mansion, and yet it felt more like home to her than any place she had ever known. The air was heavy with the scent of books, old coffee, and the faintest trace of the damp air outside. The city's distant hum echoed through the cracked windows, but the room felt peaceful, the kind of quiet that gave her room to think, to breathe.

Julian was sitting across from her, his brow furrowed in concentration as he scribbled furiously in a notebook. He had always been a man of action, his mind always racing, always thinking. His obsession with his work was palpable, and Elara had come to understand that his mind wasn't easily distracted. He was driven, but that drive was often a double-edged sword.

"You're thinking too much again," Elara said softly, her eyes tracing the lines of his face, the intensity of his focus. He looked up at her, his lips curving into a wry smile.

"I have to," he said, his voice tight with the kind of determination that Elara knew all too well. "I need to figure this out. If I can just make the connection clear enough—"

She shook her head, leaning forward. "Julian, I know how important this is to you, but it can't consume you like this. You've been obsessing over it for weeks now. You need to let it breathe."

He stared at her for a moment, the weight of her words hanging in the air. His eyes softened, but there was still that spark of determination in them, that quiet, unyielding drive that both fascinated and worried her.

"You don't understand," he said after a pause. "This isn't just about curiosity. It's more than that. I've been trying to figure this out for years, Elara. The connection... between parallel worlds. I can feel it. There's something there, something I'm not seeing. And I have to find it."

Elara couldn't deny the passion that burned in him. It was the same fire that had led him to question everything, to search for answers in places that others wouldn't dare. But she also knew that obsession, when left unchecked, could destroy everything around it. It could consume you whole, until there was nothing left but the pursuit of an idea that might never materialize.

"I get it, Julian," she said quietly. "But you can't let it control you. Not like this. There's more to life than theories, than equations. What about us? What about... everything we've started here?"

A Scientist's Obsession

His expression shifted then, a flash of vulnerability crossing his face before he masked it with a determined look.

"I'm not abandoning you, Elara," he said firmly. "I'm not going to lose myself in this. I just... need to understand it. This obsession, this drive—it's a part of me. But you're a part of me too. You've helped me see that."

The words sank into her like a balm, soothing the ache that had been gnawing at her. She wanted to believe him. She wanted to trust that he could balance this obsession with the love they were building, but a part of her couldn't shake the nagging feeling that Julian's pursuit was taking him further away from her, further from the life they could have together.

The silence between them grew thick with unspoken words. Elara could feel the weight of his focus shifting back to the notebook in his hands, the numbers and equations on the page an attempt to contain something far larger than the paper could hold. She reached out, placing a hand gently on his. He paused, his eyes meeting hers, the warmth in his gaze momentarily grounding her.

"Promise me you won't let this take you away from me," she said, her voice softer now, more vulnerable than she'd ever allowed herself to be. "Promise me that we won't be lost in your obsession."

For a long moment, Julian didn't speak. The room was alive with the tension between them, the unspoken bond that neither of them could deny. Finally, he nodded, his thumb brushing over her hand.

"I promise," he said, his voice steady. "I promise I'll find a balance. With you, Elara. Always."

The words were enough to ease some of the worry in her chest, but doubt lingered like a shadow in the back of her mind. Was it possible to find a balance between his obsession and the life they were building together? Or would Julian's pursuit of the unknown tear them apart before they even had the chance to find out?

The thought clung to her like an invisible thread, pulling at her as the days passed. Elara watched him with a mixture of longing and fear. There were moments when they were together, when he would look at her with that soft intensity, and everything seemed perfect. But then, in the quiet moments when he returned to his work, when the hours slipped by unnoticed, Elara felt a pang of isolation. She wasn't sure if he noticed, if he felt it too—the space that was beginning to grow between them, the distance that his obsession was carving out.

It wasn't just Julian's work that pulled him away from her, though. The world she had left behind was closing in on her. Her parents hadn't stopped trying to reach her, the calls and messages growing more insistent, more desperate. They were still pressuring her to return to the fold, to follow the path they had so carefully mapped out for her. And Adrian—Adrian had become a constant presence in the periphery of her life, his subtle attempts to reclaim her attention growing more frequent and more forceful. He didn't understand. None of them did.

Elara had chosen Julian, had chosen a life that was hers to shape, and yet, the more she leaned into that decision, the more she realized how fragile it all was. The balance between love and freedom, between a life untethered and one that had always been controlled—it was precarious, and she wasn't sure how long she could hold on to both.

One evening, as she sat on the couch in Julian's apartment, reading a book to distract herself from the creeping doubts, she heard the familiar sound of keys rattling at the door. She looked up just as Julian entered, his face tired, his expression strained.

"Elara," he said quietly, stepping toward her. There was something in his voice—something she hadn't heard before, a subtle undercurrent of anxiety. "I've been thinking."

She set the book aside, her heart sinking in her chest. "About?"

"The theory," he said, his hands rubbing at his temples. "It's... it's not what I thought. It's more complicated than I imagined. It's like I'm getting closer, but the closer I get, the more it feels like I'm losing touch with reality. I need to go deeper."

Elara stood, walking toward him. The tension in his voice was palpable, and she could feel her heart racing. "Julian... what are you saying?"

He looked at her, his eyes haunted, filled with something she couldn't quite name. "I need to go away. For a while. I can't explain it all yet, but I have to do this."

The words hit her like a slap. Her breath caught in her throat, the room spinning around her. She had promised herself that this wouldn't happen, that he wouldn't drift away, that they wouldn't lose each other in the pursuit of something beyond their grasp. But now, standing before her, Julian was already slipping away. His obsession had claimed him, just as she had feared.

"Julian, no," she whispered, her voice trembling. "Don't leave. Not like this."

"I have to," he said, his voice soft but resolute. "I need to find the answer. I need to know if what I'm seeing is real."

And in that moment, Elara knew. She knew that love, no matter how pure, could never exist in a fragmented world. Not without sacrifice. Not without consequences. She didn't know how much longer she could hold on, but she knew one thing for sure: this was the beginning of the end.

The beginning of the end of everything she had hoped for, everything she had fought for. Julian was slipping away, and she was powerless to stop it.

Nine

Shadows

Elara paced the small living room of Julian's apartment, her hands trembling as she ran them through her hair. The words Julian had spoken echoed in her mind, replaying over and over again, each time striking harder than the last. "I need to go away. For a while. I can't explain it all yet, but I have to do this." It had felt like a betrayal, a cruel twist of fate that had landed between them, a choice that Elara wasn't ready to accept.

She had spent the entire evening in a haze, the quiet of the apartment turning oppressive as the weight of Julian's decision settled on her shoulders. Her heart felt heavy, an anchor dragging her down into a deep, cold sea. The man she had fallen for—the one who had shown her the world outside the golden cage of her family—was slipping away. The same obsession that had drawn her to him now threatened to pull him out of her reach, and no matter how much she wanted to fight it, Elara knew there was nothing she could do to change it.

The apartment felt emptier now than it had ever been. Julian had left to "clear his head," as he had put it. And Elara was left to confront the reality of his decision alone. She could hear the faint hum of traffic outside the window, the city alive and bustling as if the world didn't care about the pain she was feeling. But for her, the world had shifted, and she was struggling to find her place in it again.

She closed her eyes and leaned her forehead against the cool glass of the window, looking out at the city she had grown up in. There was a distance between her and everything she had known, a distance that had only grown since she had met Julian. She had stepped away from her family's world, and yet it wasn't enough. It never felt like enough. The life she had tried to escape was still lingering in the background, creeping into the edges of her new reality, threatening to swallow her whole.

"Elara?"

She startled, her breath catching as she turned to see Julian standing in the doorway. His figure was silhouetted against the dim light of the hallway, and for a moment, it felt as if the world had stopped spinning. The intensity in his eyes was unmistakable, a mix of guilt, determination, and something else she couldn't quite place.

"What are you doing here?" she asked, her voice barely a whisper. She couldn't hide the hurt, the confusion that had clouded her words. She had expected him to be gone longer, maybe even to leave for good, but here he was, standing before her as if he hadn't just shattered her world.

"I needed to see you," Julian said, his voice low, his gaze unwavering. He stepped into the apartment, his footsteps slow but sure. There was an unfamiliar weight to his presence now, as if he had changed in some subtle way, like a shadow falling over him. But he was here, and that was all Elara needed to know.

"Why?" Her heart was pounding in her chest, the words tumbling out before she could stop them. "You said you needed to go away. You told me you had to leave—"

"I know," he interrupted, his voice strained. "And I meant it. But then I realized something… I can't keep running from this. I can't keep pretending that I can separate the two parts of my life. You and my work—both of them matter to me. But I've been too consumed by one. And I've hurt you in the process."

Elara's pulse quickened as she absorbed his words. She had never heard him speak like this before—so raw, so vulnerable. And yet, there was still that flicker of something else behind his eyes. Something she couldn't quite identify, something that felt like a warning. He wasn't just talking about his work, about his obsession with the theories he had spent years unraveling. There was something more at play, something that he wasn't saying, something that felt like it could destroy everything.

"You can't just turn this around, Julian," she said, her voice breaking. "I can't keep waiting for you to choose me, for you to choose a life outside of your obsession. You promised me you wouldn't let it take you away from me, but here we are. Again."

His gaze faltered, but only for a moment. Then he took a step closer, his hand reaching out toward her. "I never wanted to hurt you, Elara. I swear. I thought I could balance it, but I was wrong. I thought if I could just finish this one thing, if I could just make the breakthrough, everything would make sense. But I was wrong."

She swallowed hard, stepping back, the weight of his words pressing against her chest. She wanted to believe him. She wanted to believe that he wasn't the man he had been just days ago—lost in his work, consumed by the need to solve the puzzle that had driven him for years. But something had shifted. She could feel it in the air between them, like the ground beneath her feet was cracking, threatening to swallow her whole.

"You say you want this, Julian," she whispered, her voice trembling. "You say you want to be with me, but how can I trust that? How can I trust you if you can't even trust yourself?"

He didn't answer immediately, and in that silence, Elara felt the distance between them widen. The man who had once promised her that he wouldn't let his obsession tear them apart was no longer the man standing before her. Something was different. He had changed, and she wasn't sure if she recognized him anymore.

"I've been chasing something for so long," Julian said finally, his voice quiet, almost haunted. "Something I thought would explain everything—the missing link, the truth that would tie it all together. But all this time, I've been chasing shadows. I've been chasing a life that wasn't real. I lost sight of what really matters. I lost sight of you."

Elara felt the sting of his words, the way they struck deep inside her. She wanted to be angry. She wanted to scream at him for all the pain he had caused her, for all the ways he had pulled away, for all the ways he had kept her on the edge of his life without ever truly letting her in. But as she looked at him, standing there with that look in his eyes, she realized something. She was still holding on. She was still hoping. Hoping that he would choose her, hoping that he would be the man he once seemed to be—the man who had shown her what it was like to be truly seen, truly understood.

"I don't know if I can keep doing this, Julian," Elara said, her voice barely above a whisper. She could feel the weight of her own words settling over her like a shroud. "I don't know if I can keep living in the shadow of your obsession. I can't keep waiting for you to choose me when you're already so lost in your work."

He took a step closer to her, his hand reaching out, but Elara instinctively pulled away. "I am choosing you," he said, his voice full of conviction. "I don't want to lose you. I don't want to lose us."

But Elara couldn't shake the feeling that she had already lost him. That whatever connection they had shared, whatever bond had once seemed unbreakable, was slipping away, piece by piece. His obsession had claimed him in a way that no love, no promise, could ever compete with. And no matter how much she wanted to fight for them, she wasn't sure she had the strength to fight against something that had taken over his mind, his soul.

"I need to figure this out, Elara," Julian continued, his voice softer now, pleading. "I can't just walk away from it. But I want you to know that you are my priority. You are. I just… I need time."

Elara stood there, her heart torn in two. She could feel the tears welling up in her eyes, the heaviness of the moment pressing down on her chest. She had never felt more lost in her entire life. She had chosen him, she had given him everything, and yet, here she was, standing on the precipice of losing it all.

"I can't wait forever," she said quietly, her voice breaking. "I can't wait for you to decide if I'm worth it."

The silence that followed was suffocating, thick with unsaid words, with emotions that neither of them was brave enough to face. Julian opened his mouth, but no words came out. He simply stood there, his expression unreadable, the distance between them widening with every passing second.

And in that moment, Elara realized something she had been unwilling to admit to herself: She couldn't save him. She couldn't fix him. She couldn't make him choose her. No matter how much she loved him, no matter how much she wanted

Shadows

their love to be enough, it wasn't. Not if he couldn't choose to let go of the shadows that had haunted him for so long.

And so, with a broken heart and a quiet, painful resolve, Elara turned and walked away. She couldn't stay in this fractured world. Not anymore. Not when the man she had given everything to was lost to a world of shadows.

And as she left him standing in the doorway, she knew that whatever happened next, the world she had known—the one she had left behind—would never be the same again.

Ten

The Kiss

⁓৹ঔ৹⁓

Clara sat in the darkened corner of the cafe, the warm cup of tea in her hands cooling as she absently stirred it. She had found herself here several times over the past few days, escaping the overwhelming silence of Julian's apartment, the oppressive expectations of her family, and the looming pressure of everything she had tried to leave behind. The café was small, nestled in a quiet street far from the chaos of the city's main roads, and it had become her refuge. The clinking of cups, the low murmur of conversations, the smell of freshly ground coffee—it all created a cocoon of normalcy that she so desperately needed.

But today, even this sanctuary felt too small, too suffocating. Her mind kept returning to the same question: What now? She had walked away from Julian, from the man who had ignited something inside her, something that was both exhilarating and terrifying. But as the days stretched into silence, she couldn't help but wonder if she had made the right choice.

Her thoughts were interrupted by the sudden opening of the café door. A sharp gust of wind blew in with a figure, causing the door to slam shut behind them. Elara barely looked up, the familiar weight of the world pulling her focus back to her cup. But then, she felt it. A shift in the air. She could feel the change before she even saw him.

A shadow fell over her table.

"Is this seat taken?" The voice was low, familiar. Elara froze, her heart skipping a beat, before her gaze slowly lifted to meet the person standing before her.

Julian.

He looked different, yet the same. The same intensity in his eyes, the same quiet confidence in the way he held himself. But there was something new in the way he looked at her—something darker, more conflicted. His expression was a mixture of longing and regret, a silent apology hanging between them that neither of them knew how to speak aloud.

"I thought you were…" Elara began, her voice trembling despite herself. "I thought you were done with this."

Julian didn't answer immediately. Instead, he sat down across from her, his eyes never leaving hers. For a moment, the world around them seemed to disappear, the soft murmur of the café fading into nothingness as they were caught in a moment of suspended time.

"I thought so too," he said, his voice barely above a whisper. "But I can't keep pretending. Not anymore. Elara, I've been trying to run from this thing between us, trying to convince myself that it's just a distraction, a fleeting thing. But every time I try to turn away, I end up back here. With you."

The words hung in the air, heavier than any of them had ever been. Elara's heart beat erratically in her chest, but she fought to keep her composure, fighting the urge to reach out, to touch him, to ask him for the answers that she didn't even know how to voice.

"What do you want, Julian?" she asked, her voice quieter now, steadier than it had been in days. "I can't keep doing this. I can't keep being this... uncertainty in your life."

Julian's eyes softened, and for a moment, he looked vulnerable, unsure of what to say. But his words came with a quiet strength that made her feel like the world was shifting again, this time toward something she wasn't sure she could stop.

"I want you," he said simply. "But I don't know how to reconcile that with everything else. The work, the obsession—it's always been there. But so have you. And for once, I want to make a choice. A real one."

Elara felt a rush of emotions flood her—relief, anger, fear, and desire all blending together in a storm she didn't know how to navigate. She wanted to believe him. She wanted to trust that he was being honest with her, that the man in front of her was the same person who had made her feel seen in ways she never thought possible. But her doubt, the nagging fear that had been growing inside her, kept her from taking that leap.

"I don't know if I can believe you anymore," she said, her voice trembling despite the effort to sound firm. "You said you needed time. You said you had to figure it out. And now you're telling me you've made a choice? How can I trust that? How can I trust you?"

Julian's face fell, the rawness of her words striking him harder than any harsh words could. He reached across the table, his hand hovering just over hers, but he didn't touch her. Not yet. It felt like the air between them was too thick, too fragile for a touch that could mean everything or nothing at all.

"I'm not asking you to trust me blindly," he said, his voice rough with emotion. "I'm asking you to give me a chance to prove it. To show you that I can make this work. That we can make this work."

Elara's heart beat faster. She could see the sincerity in his eyes, but she could also feel the distance between them, the invisible wall that had been erected over the past few days. She wanted to reach out, to take his hand, to let him pull her into the warmth of his promise. But the fear—fear of getting hurt, fear of losing herself again—kept her anchored to the table.

For a long moment, they sat in silence, the weight of everything hanging between them. The café, once a haven, now felt like a prison, the air thick with unspoken words. Elara looked down at her hands, trying to calm the storm inside her. She didn't know what she wanted anymore. She didn't know if she was strong enough to face the man who had so effortlessly torn her heart in two. And yet, despite the confusion, despite the ache in her chest, she couldn't bring herself to push him away.

"I can't promise you that I'm ready," Elara finally whispered. "But I can't walk away either."

Julian didn't need to hear anything more. Without another word, he reached out and gently cupped her face in his hands. It was a simple gesture, yet it held more weight than any promise he could ever make. His thumb brushed across her cheek, and for a fleeting moment, everything in the world felt like it was aligning.

"Elara," he whispered, his voice thick with emotion, "I never wanted to hurt you. I never wanted to pull you into this world, but I can't let you go. Not without fighting for you."

Before she could answer, before she could let the words settle between them, he leaned in. His lips brushed against hers, light and hesitant at first, like the soft touch of a storm approaching. The kiss was everything and nothing all at once. It was the culmination of everything they had been through, everything they had felt. It was the kiss of a man who had been lost and was finally finding his way, and of a woman who was still torn between the love she had found and the life she had left behind.

The Kiss

The world seemed to stop. The noise of the café faded. The tension, the anger, the fear—all of it was swept away in the quiet intimacy of the kiss. It wasn't perfect. It wasn't the fairy tale kiss that would solve all of their problems, but in that moment, Elara felt something she hadn't felt in days: hope. Maybe it was foolish, maybe it was reckless, but for once, she wasn't afraid of it. She wasn't afraid of the chaos, of the uncertainty.

Julian pulled back, his forehead resting against hers as they both tried to catch their breath. "We can figure this out," he murmured. "Together."

For the first time in what felt like forever, Elara believed him. She didn't have all the answers. She didn't know what would come next, or if they could truly make this work. But she didn't need to know. Not anymore. In that kiss, she had found something—something worth fighting for. And for the first time, she was ready to fight for it.

"Together," she whispered back.

And in that moment, it didn't matter that the world outside had fallen apart. It didn't matter that the life she had known was slipping through her fingers. What mattered was that she wasn't alone anymore.

Eleven

Fabric of Time

The night was heavy with the scent of rain, the air thick with the promise of a storm. Elara stood by the window of Julian's apartment, watching the droplets streak down the glass as if they were racing each other to the ground. Her thoughts were a swirling storm of their own, too chaotic to make sense of. She had promised herself that she wouldn't look back and regret the choices she had made, but the more she tried to move forward, the more the weight of the past seemed to drag her back.

It had been a week since their kiss—it had felt like a resolution, a promise of something real, something worth fighting for. But now, with Julian away on one of his "research trips" that had become more frequent, Elara was left to grapple with the uncertainty of their situation. She had tried to convince herself that she could trust him, that his promise to fight for her was enough, but every passing hour without him felt like a betrayal in itself.

The door to the apartment creaked open, snapping Elara from her reverie. She turned just in time to see Julian enter, his rain-soaked coat hanging off his shoulders, his hair damp and sticking to his forehead. His eyes met hers immediately, the exhaustion in them unmistakable, but so was the determination. He had come back, and Elara couldn't help but feel a rush of relief, tempered by the unease that had followed her ever since he left.

"Elara," he said, his voice strained, as though the simple word held more weight than he could express.

She didn't say anything right away, just watched as he shook the rain off his coat and hung it up by the door. She could see the tension in his posture, the way his hands trembled ever so slightly as he peeled off his shoes and made his way toward her. There was something about his movements, a certain hesitance, that made her chest tighten with an unfamiliar kind of dread.

"You've been gone for days," she said finally, her voice quiet but firm. "I thought you were… I thought we were past this. What happened?"

Julian paused for a moment, his eyes flickering with something she couldn't quite read. He looked as though he wanted to say something, but the words seemed to get stuck in his throat. The space between them felt heavier with every passing second, and Elara hated it. She hated that she felt like an outsider in her own life, like the connection they had built was slowly unraveling.

"I had to go back," Julian said, his voice quieter now. "I needed to finish something. Something that—" He cut himself off, as if he wasn't sure how much to say, or even if he should say anything at all.

Elara's heart sank as she watched him. He was lying, she could tell. He had promised her that he would stop running, that he would focus on their future. And yet, here he was again—distant, elusive, hiding something from her. She had thought she had known him, that their connection was strong enough to withstand the storms of his obsession, but now, it felt like that connection was starting to fray at the edges.

"Julian," she said, her voice hardening despite herself. "What aren't you telling me?"

He didn't answer right away, his eyes darting around the room as though he were searching for an escape. His jaw clenched, and Elara could see the conflict inside him, the war between the man she had fallen for and the one who had spent years chasing after theories that might never lead to anything. She could feel the walls he had built around himself, the ones that had kept her out even when she had given him everything.

"I'm sorry," Julian said at last, his voice breaking slightly. "I should have been honest with you. But this—what I'm working on, it's bigger than anything I've ever done before. It's not just about finding the answer anymore. It's about something else, something I can't explain. I thought I could compartmentalize it, but now I'm starting to think that I can't."

Elara's pulse quickened. She took a step closer to him, her eyes narrowing. "What do you mean? What have you been working on?"

Julian hesitated again, and for the first time, Elara saw something in his eyes that made her stomach churn. Fear. A kind of fear she had never seen in him before.

"I've found something, Elara," he whispered, barely audible. "Something that I can't ignore. I think I've figured out how to… how to break through. But it's not just a theory anymore. I'm starting to believe that the worlds, the dimensions—they aren't as separate as we've been led to believe. There's a way to—"

"To what?" Elara interrupted, her breath caught in her throat. "To open a door between them?"

Julian's eyes locked onto hers, and for the first time, she saw the full weight of what he had been carrying. The exhaustion, the obsession, the desperation—all of it was there, laid bare for her to see. "I think so," he said quietly. "I think I've found a way to break through the fabric of time itself. To see the other side."

Elara stepped back, the words hitting her like a slap. "What do you mean, break through the fabric of time? Julian, this isn't a game. This is real life we're talking about. If you keep chasing after this, you'll lose everything. You'll lose us."

Julian looked as though her words physically pained him, as though the weight of the truth was too much to bear. He ran a hand through his hair, his eyes shifting uneasily.

"I can't stop now," he said, his voice barely above a whisper. "I've come too far, Elara. I can't let it go."

Elara felt the familiar pang of helplessness rising in her chest. She had known this would happen. She had known that his obsession would one day consume him, that the man she had fallen in love with would become a shadow of himself, lost in something he couldn't control. She had tried to warn him, tried to hold on to the part of him that had cared for her, but now, it seemed like she was losing him piece by piece.

"Then you've already lost me," she said, her voice breaking with the weight of her own words. "I can't keep doing this, Julian. I can't keep watching you slip away into something that doesn't even make sense. This isn't real. You're chasing ghosts."

His face hardened, the vulnerability from before quickly replaced by a mask of resolve. He took a step toward her, his expression intense, almost desperate. "I don't want to lose you," he said fiercely, his voice trembling. "But I can't give up on this. Not now. Not when I'm so close."

Elara felt a knot tighten in her chest. He was slipping further and further away from her, his obsession pulling him into a world that she couldn't follow. She had been living in the space between two realities for so long now, and she didn't know how much longer she could keep fighting for something that was slipping through her fingers.

"Then we're done," Elara said softly, her voice steady despite the storm brewing inside her. "If this is more important than what we have, then I can't keep holding on to you."

Julian flinched, his expression faltering for a split second, but then it was gone, replaced by the stubborn resolve that had defined him for so long. "I'm sorry," he whispered, his voice hoarse with emotion. "I never meant for it to be this way. I never meant for you to feel like this. But I can't stop. I can't."

With that, he turned and walked away, the door clicking shut behind him with finality. Elara stood there, frozen, her heart beating erratically in her chest as the silence in the apartment pressed down on her. The weight of his absence was suffocating, more so than any of the fears she had faced. She knew, in that moment, that she had lost him.

She had chosen love, and in doing so, she had lost the man she had fallen for. The man who had promised her everything, but who had given in to something he could never control.

And as the storm raged outside, Elara realized the truth. Julian had never truly been hers to keep. And the rift between their worlds was no longer just theoretical. It was real. And it had torn them apart.

Twelve

Unseen Connection

Elara stood in the doorway of Julian's apartment, the space between them wide and growing wider with each passing second. The world felt heavy in the silence that hung between them, a suffocating tension that neither of them seemed willing to break. His figure was still framed in the doorway, the rain outside drumming steadily against the windows, a constant reminder of the storm that had come with the night.

"I told you I couldn't stop," Julian's voice broke through the stillness, rough with emotion, his words hanging in the air like a challenge, a plea, a confession. "I never meant to hurt you, Elara. I never wanted to hurt anyone, but this thing, this research, it's pulling me under, and I can't get out."

Her heart raced, pounding against her chest as she tried to

steady herself, to gather her thoughts, to make sense of the words he had just spoken. She wanted to scream, to tell him how foolish he was to choose an obsession over her, over them. But the words wouldn't come. Not yet.

"You think I don't understand?" Elara finally said, her voice shaking with restrained anger. "I do understand, Julian. But do you understand me? Do you understand what it feels like to stand here, watching you slip further away with every single word you say? Watching you lose yourself to something that's killing you?"

Julian flinched, the rawness in his eyes flashing like a wound too deep to heal. He ran a hand through his hair, frustration, guilt, and sorrow warring within him. "I never wanted this to happen. I didn't ask for this obsession, Elara. It came to me like a whisper in the dark. And now, now I can't escape it. It's all I think about. It's all that matters."

"And what about me?" Elara's voice cracked, the dam inside her breaking. "What about the life we were building? The one I believed in? Was that just a momentary distraction? Was it just another thing you could walk away from the minute it got difficult?"

Julian's face darkened with the weight of her words, but it was as though something in him snapped, a subtle shift in his demeanor as his eyes locked onto hers. The guilt, the pain, the uncertainty—all of it was laid bare in the rawness of his expression. "Elara," he whispered her name like a prayer. "Please. Don't walk away from me now. I can't lose you, not like this."

The storm outside seemed to grow louder, the wind whipping against the glass as if nature itself was amplifying the chaos in their hearts. Elara swallowed, her throat tight with the fight she had been holding back, the fight that she was no longer sure she had the strength to continue.

She turned away from him, her hand pressed against the cool surface of the wall for support. The words she needed to say were caught in her throat, tangled in the raw pain of what she was feeling. What had she become in his eyes? A fleeting distraction, a casualty of his obsession? Or had she truly mattered to him?

Her breath caught in her chest as she heard Julian approach her from behind. His steps were slow, measured, as if giving her space to breathe, to make a decision she was incapable of making. He was afraid of her leaving. And yet, in some way, he had already left her. His mind, his heart, his soul—he had already abandoned her in favor of something bigger than both of them. Something that would consume him, regardless of the cost.

"Elara," Julian said, his voice low and filled with a desperate tenderness that sent a wave of conflicting emotions crashing over her. "I can't undo what I've done. I can't make up for the time I've lost or the hurt I've caused. But I'm asking you to stay with me. To help me find my way back. I can't do this alone."

Her pulse quickened, the raw ache of wanting him, wanting

to fix him, warring with the realization that maybe this wasn't something she could fix. Maybe the man she had once loved was beyond reach. Beyond repair.

"Can you hear yourself?" Elara turned, her voice sharper than she had intended. "You're asking me to save you, Julian, but you don't even know if you want to be saved. You're still lost in this world you've built, still chasing after something you don't fully understand. And I... I don't know if I can keep watching you destroy yourself."

Julian stood motionless for a moment, the weight of her words sinking in. His face was pale, a reflection of the turmoil that twisted within him. He had never been this vulnerable, this unsure. He had always been the one in control, the scientist, the researcher, the man who could see patterns in chaos. But now, in front of her, he was nothing more than a man who was terrified of losing the one thing that had ever truly mattered.

"Elara," he began, his voice raw, "I never wanted this. I never wanted to be this person. I've spent so many years trying to piece together the fabric of time, to make sense of everything that has happened. But I see now that I've torn everything apart, including us. Please don't leave me now. Please."

Her heart ached for him, for the man he had been and the man he was becoming. She could feel the pull between them, the connection that had once been unbreakable. But something had shifted, something had broken, and Elara wasn't sure if she could ever put the pieces of them back together.

"Maybe I'm not the one who can save you, Julian," she said softly, her voice trembling with the weight of her own helplessness. "Maybe you have to save yourself first."

The words lingered in the air, thick with finality. For a moment, neither of them spoke, the silence between them heavy with unspoken truths. Elara's mind raced as she tried to make sense of it all. She had loved him. She had given him everything. But now, the man who stood before her was someone she didn't fully recognize. And as much as she still cared for him, she knew that she couldn't keep waiting for him to change, to choose her. Not when he couldn't even choose himself.

Julian stepped closer, his hands reaching for her, but Elara pulled back, the fear in her heart now matching the uncertainty in his eyes.

"I'm not leaving you, Julian," she whispered, her voice barely audible. "I'm leaving the man you've become."

The words hit him like a physical blow, and Elara saw the flicker of devastation in his eyes before it was quickly masked by the stoic mask he had perfected over the years. But it was too late. She had already made her decision. She could see it now, see the cracks in the foundation they had built, the irreparable damage that his obsession had caused.

"I can't fix this," she whispered, more to herself than to him. "Not anymore."

Julian stood frozen, his face unreadable. The vulnerability that had once been so apparent in him now seemed buried beneath a layer of hardened resolve. He was a man lost in the storm of his own making, and Elara realized with a heavy heart that he might never find his way back to her.

"I'm sorry," Julian said quietly, his voice almost breaking. "I never wanted to lose you."

Elara's heart shattered, the finality of his words cutting through her like a knife. She could feel the tears threatening to fall, but she held them back. She couldn't cry. Not now. Not when she knew that what they had was slipping through her fingers like sand.

With a final glance at Julian, Elara turned away, walking toward the door. She couldn't stay in this fractured world anymore. She couldn't keep chasing after a love that was no longer hers to keep.

As she stepped out into the rain, her heart felt heavier than it ever had before. The storm that raged outside seemed to mirror the chaos inside her, but Elara knew this was the only way forward. She had to let go. She had to walk away, no matter how much it hurt. Because sometimes, the greatest act of love was knowing when to let go.

And as the rain soaked through her clothes and the cold wind cut through her skin, Elara realized the truth. She couldn't keep living in the rift between their worlds. Not anymore.

Thirteen

The Watchers

Elara's footsteps echoed in the empty street as she walked away from Julian's apartment, the sound a sharp reminder of the void that had opened between them. The rain had slowed to a light drizzle, but the air still felt thick, heavy with the weight of her decision. Each drop that hit the ground seemed to punctuate her thoughts, each one a tiny, insistent reminder of the path she had chosen.

She didn't look back. She couldn't. She had walked away from him once, but this time felt different. It felt final. The door she had closed behind her wasn't one she could reopen. The connection that had once burned so brightly between them had faded, and though a part of her wanted to reach out and bring it back to life, she knew deep down that it was beyond repair.

The city around her felt distant, muted, as if the world had fallen into a quiet, uneasy sleep. The streets were deserted, save for the occasional car speeding by, its headlights casting long shadows on the pavement. Elara kept walking, the weight of her decision heavy on her chest. There was no turning back, no way to undo the pain, the heartbreak that had been created. She had given Julian everything, and in the end, he had chosen his obsession over her, over them.

As she walked, her thoughts drifted to what he had said—his words about the "rift," about the other side, about dimensions and time. She couldn't help but feel a cold shiver run down her spine. What if he was right? What if there was something on the other side? What if everything he had been chasing wasn't just a product of his obsession but something real? Something that could change everything?

Her breath hitched at the thought. But no. She couldn't afford to let herself get lost in his theories again. She had to focus on the here and now. She had to focus on herself, on her own life, on the future she had been so carefully crafting for herself before Julian had come into it. She couldn't lose herself to the unknown.

As she neared the entrance to the alleyway that led to her apartment, a familiar voice called out to her from behind.

"Elara!"

She froze, her body tensing at the sound. Her heart began to pound in her chest as she turned, almost hoping that it wasn't who she thought it was. But when she saw him standing there, his silhouette dark against the backdrop of the streetlights, her heart sank.

Adrian.

He was dressed in his usual pristine suit, his features sharp, his posture unyielding as he approached her. There was no warmth in his eyes, no kindness in his expression—just the cold, calculating look of a man who was used to getting what he wanted. And he wanted her. He always had.

"Elara," he said again, his voice like ice. "I've been looking for you."

She forced herself to remain calm, her pulse still racing from the encounter with Julian, from the turmoil inside her. She took a deep breath, trying to steady herself as she faced him. "What do you want, Adrian?"

"I think you know why I'm here," he said, his eyes narrowing as he took a step closer. "You've been avoiding me. I've tried reaching out, but you haven't returned any of my calls. I think it's time we had a conversation."

Elara's stomach turned. The last thing she wanted right now was to deal with Adrian, to be dragged back into the world she had been desperately trying to escape. She could feel the anger rising inside her, the need to lash out, to make him understand that she wasn't the woman he thought she was. But she knew better than to engage with him. Adrian was a master manipulator. He knew how to twist words, how to make people bend to his will. She had spent years trying to fight him, to resist his advances, but she couldn't do it anymore. Not like this.

"I don't have time for this, Adrian," she said, her voice tight, cold. "I've made my decision."

He laughed, a humorless sound that echoed through the alleyway. "You think this is about your decisions? You're not the one who's making the decisions here, Elara. Your family has already decided for you. And you're not going to get away that easily."

Her heart skipped a beat as the words sank in. "What are you talking about?"

He stepped closer, his gaze darkening as he reached out to touch her arm, his fingers cold against her skin. "You've made your choice, haven't you? You've chosen him. That fool. The one with the wild theories and the obsession with things he doesn't even understand. But what you don't realize, Elara, is that your family will never let you go. Not like this. You're too important to them. Too valuable."

"What are you saying?" Her voice trembled despite herself. "This isn't about my family. This is about me, my life. I'm choosing my own path."

Adrian's lips curled into a sneer. "You think you're choosing your own path, but you're still walking down the road they've laid out for you. You can't escape it. You can't escape what you are. And neither can he."

Her heart raced as his words hit her like a brick. She had been trying so hard to push away the truth, to deny the role her family had played in her life, but Adrian's words pierced through the layers of denial. No matter what she did, she couldn't escape them. She couldn't escape the legacy they had built for her. The rift between her and her family wasn't just a divide in her heart; it was a chasm that could never be crossed.

"What does that mean?" she asked, her voice barely more than a whisper.

Adrian smiled, a dark, knowing smile that sent a chill down her spine. "You'll see soon enough, Elara. Your little escape from your family's grasp? It's just a phase. It's just a brief moment before they reel you back in."

Before Elara could respond, Adrian turned and started walking away, his coat swirling behind him as he disappeared into the darkness. She stood frozen in place, her mind reeling with the implications of his words. What had he meant? What was he talking about?

She turned back toward her apartment, her thoughts clouded with the weight of his words and the lingering fear that something bigger was at play. Something that she couldn't yet understand.

As she reached her front door, the feeling of being watched crept over her again. She couldn't shake the sensation that there were eyes on her, hidden in the shadows. The realization hit her like a bolt of lightning: She wasn't just being pulled between Julian and her family. There was something else out there, something darker, something waiting for her to make the wrong move.

The door to her apartment clicked open, but she didn't immediately step inside. Her gaze shifted to the shadows around her—at the edge of the alley, at the corners of the street. Was it just her imagination, or was someone watching her?

She shook the thought away, trying to brush off the unease that had settled deep within her chest. But she couldn't escape the feeling that the world around her was shifting, that the rift Julian had spoken of was more than just a metaphor—it was real. And she was caught in the middle of it.

As she stepped into the apartment and closed the door behind her, Elara glanced out of the window, her mind racing with the implications of the night. The city stretched out before her, its lights twinkling like distant stars. And somewhere, hidden within the darkness, she knew there were forces at work that she couldn't yet understand. Forces that were watching her, waiting for her to make the wrong move.

And as she stood there, alone in the silence of her apartment, Elara realized that the rift between her and the life she had known was only the beginning. The real danger, the real threat, was still waiting in the shadows, watching, waiting for her to make her next move. And when she did, she knew, everything would change forever.

Fourteen

Falling Through Reality

The air was thick with tension as Elara stood in the center of her apartment, her heart pounding like a drum in her chest. The encounter with Adrian had left her unsettled, his cryptic words echoing in her mind, creating ripples of unease that she couldn't shake. He had always been a constant presence in her life, one that she had learned to resist, but this time felt different. His words about her family and her future were not just threats—they felt like something far more dangerous.

She turned toward the window, her gaze fixed on the city that stretched out before her, its lights twinkling in the distance like distant stars. For a moment, it seemed peaceful, almost serene. But beneath that calm surface, something was shifting—something she couldn't fully understand, something that was pulling her deeper into a world she had never asked to be part of.

Her thoughts shifted back to Julian. The storm of emotions that had surrounded their last meeting still raged inside her. The kiss they had shared, the promises they had made—it had all felt so real, so solid. But now, with the weight of Adrian's words and the growing tension in her own heart, Elara couldn't shake the feeling that she was being pulled in two directions, neither of which seemed like a safe place to be.

The phone buzzed in her hand, snapping her out of her thoughts. She glanced at the screen, her heart leaping in her chest when she saw that it was a message from Julian.

"Can we meet? I need to explain everything."

She stared at the message for a long moment, the words swimming before her eyes. She wanted to respond, to agree to meet him, to somehow make sense of the confusion that had taken over her life. But something held her back. She had given so much of herself to Julian, allowed herself to believe in the life they could have together, and yet, every time she tried to move forward, the past seemed to come rushing back, tearing at the fragile bond they had built.

The phone buzzed again, another message from Julian:

"Please, Elara. I swear this is important. I'm not asking for forgiveness. I just need you to understand. Please meet me."

Elara closed her eyes, her fingers hovering over the keys as she debated what to do. She wanted to trust him. She wanted to believe that they could still find a way to make this work, that the connection they had shared was something worth fighting for. But after everything that had happened—after the way he had pulled away from her, the way he had become consumed by his work, by his obsession with the rift—Elara wasn't sure if she could keep holding on.

She felt the familiar weight of doubt settling in her chest, threatening to crush her. Was it too late? Had she already lost him? Was she simply a part of his theory now, a pawn in a game that she didn't understand?

Her mind raced with questions she couldn't answer, and she knew that she had to make a choice. She couldn't keep living in the limbo of indecision. She had to decide whether to face the man she had once loved, to confront the truth of what had happened between them, or to walk away, to finally sever the connection that had bound her to him.

Taking a deep breath, Elara tapped out a response:

"Where?"

A few moments later, a new message popped up on the screen:

"Meet me at the old observatory. I'll be waiting."

Her fingers tightened around the phone as she read the message again. The observatory. It was a place they had visited together once, years ago, when their connection had been simple and uncomplicated. It had been a quiet, peaceful place where they could escape the noise of the world and simply be.

But now, the thought of returning there filled her with unease. The observatory, once a place of solace, had become something else in her mind—a place where their relationship had shifted, where the rift had begun to grow between them. It had been the first time Julian had spoken of his theories in detail, the first time he had tried to explain the pull he felt toward the rift. And it had been the moment she had realized that he would never be able to walk away from it.

She stared at the phone, torn between the desire to find closure and the fear of what she might uncover. The messages had sounded desperate, almost frantic, and for a moment, she wondered if she was walking into something that she wasn't prepared to face.

But the pull was too strong. The need for answers was too great.

With a final, resolute breath, Elara made up her mind. She grabbed her jacket and left the apartment, the door clicking shut behind her with a finality that seemed to echo in the empty space. The city outside was quieter than usual, the streets wet from the rain, the reflections of the streetlights shimmering on the pavement like ghosts.

As she made her way to the observatory, Elara couldn't shake the feeling that something was wrong. Her instincts, the ones that had served her so well in the past, were telling her that this meeting wasn't going to be what she expected. That Julian had something to reveal to her—something she wasn't ready to hear.

When she reached the observatory, the door was slightly ajar, as if Julian had been waiting for her. She pushed it open carefully, her heart racing with anticipation and dread. The room was dark, the only light coming from the faint glow of the city below, casting long shadows across the walls.

"Julian?" Elara's voice broke the silence, her words heavy with uncertainty. She stepped further into the room, her eyes scanning the shadows for any sign of him.

"I'm here," came his voice from the far side of the room, barely audible, almost as though it was a whisper carried by the wind.

Elara turned toward the sound, her breath catching in her throat as she saw him standing near the large telescope, his back to her. He was holding something in his hands, something that gleamed faintly in the dim light.

"What's going on, Julian?" she asked, her voice shaking despite her attempt to stay calm. "Why did you ask me to come here?"

He didn't turn around immediately, and for a moment, the silence between them felt oppressive. It was as if the weight of everything they had been through was too much to bear, and neither of them knew how to bridge the gap that had grown between them.

Finally, Julian spoke, his voice barely above a whisper. "I've found something, Elara. Something that could change everything."

Elara's heart skipped a beat, her body frozen in place. "What are you talking about? What could possibly change everything?"

He turned slowly, and Elara saw the look in his eyes—something she had never seen before. It wasn't the man she had fallen in love with, the one who had promised her everything. This was a man consumed by something far darker, something far more dangerous.

"I've found the key," Julian said, his voice trembling with the weight of his discovery. "The key to the rift. To the other side."

Elara felt a chill run down her spine. "What do you mean, the key?" she asked, her voice barely a whisper.

He stepped forward, his eyes locked onto hers with an intensity that made her heart race. "It's real, Elara. The other side. The dimensions. I've found a way to reach them. To bridge the gap."

Her breath caught in her throat. "No. No, Julian, this isn't what we agreed on. This isn't what you promised."

He reached out, his hand trembling as he touched her arm. "I'm so close, Elara. You have to understand. This is the breakthrough I've been searching for. And I need you to help me."

She stepped back, her heart pounding, the fear rising inside her like a tidal wave. "I can't help you with this," she said, her voice shaking. "You're chasing something that isn't real. Something that could destroy everything."

He looked at her, his expression torn. "I didn't want this. But I can't stop now. I need to know. We need to know. The rift is real, Elara. And we can change everything."

The words hit her like a blow. The rift, the dimensions, the other side—it was all real. And Julian, the man she had loved, had become so consumed by his obsession with it that he was willing to risk everything—his life, her life, their future—for the chance to reach it.

And in that moment, Elara realized that the man she had fallen in love with had already fallen through reality. He was no longer the person she had known. And she was left standing on the edge of the unknown, with no idea how to bring him back.

Fifteen

Love Beyond Equations

The air in the observatory felt thick with the weight of Julian's words, pressing down on Elara like a suffocating force. She stood there, frozen, her mind struggling to comprehend what Julian had just said. The rift is real. The other side. We can change everything. His voice echoed in her ears, each word burning with a desperation that was all too familiar.

The room seemed to close in on her, the observatory walls feeling smaller, more oppressive. The city lights below twinkled like a distant dream, and yet, in the silence of the night, it was as though the entire world had gone still. Everything had changed in an instant. Julian, the man who had once made her feel alive, who had shown her a world beyond the confines of her family's control, had become someone else—someone lost in the pursuit of something she couldn't begin to understand.

The Fortune She Didn't Want

Her gaze shifted to the large telescope in the corner of the room, its lens pointed outward into the vast, unyielding night. Julian had always spoken of it with such passion, a fascination for the stars and the mysteries of the universe that had seemed to pull him further and further away from her. But this? This was different. This wasn't just about the stars. This was about something far darker, something more dangerous.

"Elara," Julian said, his voice softer now, almost pleading. "I need you to understand. I never wanted to drag you into this. I never wanted to pull you away from everything that was real. But what I've found—it's not just a theory anymore. It's real. The rift. It's real."

She took a step back, her eyes never leaving him. He was standing in front of her now, his face pale, his hands shaking ever so slightly as he reached out to her. She could see the intensity in his eyes, the fire that had driven him to this moment, but there was something else there too—something darker, something that terrified her.

"No," Elara said, her voice steady despite the fear that gnawed at her insides. "This isn't real, Julian. This is your obsession. This is you, losing yourself to something you can't control."

The silence that followed her words was deafening. Julian looked at her, his brow furrowed in confusion, as if her refusal to believe him didn't make sense. He had always been driven, but this? This was different. She could see it in the way his eyes burned, the way he clung to this idea like a lifeline.

"Elara, please," Julian said, his voice breaking. "I don't know how else to explain it. I've been studying it for months. Years. I've made connections, found patterns in the fabric of time, the dimensions. I've seen glimpses of it—of the other side. I know it's real. And I know I'm close."

Elara's breath caught in her throat, and she took another step back, shaking her head as she tried to make sense of it. "What other side, Julian? What are you talking about? You're chasing shadows. You're chasing something that doesn't exist."

"I've seen it," Julian said, his voice becoming more urgent. "I've felt it, Elara. The rift is real. I can see the threads that tie everything together. The past, the future, the parallel worlds… it's all connected. And if I can just reach it—if I can just unlock it—we can change everything. We can fix everything."

Her mind reeled as she tried to process his words. Change everything? Fix everything? What did he mean by that? Her chest tightened with panic, and she couldn't keep up with the whirlwind of thoughts that spun through her mind.

"Fix everything?" Elara echoed, her voice rising. "What are you talking about, Julian? What could you possibly fix by tearing apart the fabric of reality? You're playing with something you don't understand! You don't know what the consequences are!"

Julian's face hardened, and for a moment, Elara saw a flash of something she hadn't seen before—something dark and unrecognizable. He was no longer the man she had fallen in love with. He was someone else, someone consumed by the very thing that had once made him so alluring to her. His obsession was all-encompassing, and she realized, too late, that she had been drawn into it, entangled in his web of equations and theories, of dreams and promises that now seemed like nothing more than illusions.

"I can't stop now, Elara," Julian said, his voice cold with finality. "I've come too far. The rift is the answer. It's everything. It's not just about me anymore. It's about us—our future, our existence. I know you're scared. I know you don't understand, but I need you to trust me."

Her heart raced in her chest, the panic rising like a tidal wave. Trust him? How could she trust him when he was so lost in his own delusions, when he was willing to risk everything—their love, their future, their very reality—for something she couldn't even comprehend?

"No, Julian," Elara whispered, shaking her head as she stepped away from him. "I can't trust you. Not like this."

He took a step forward, his hand reaching out for her, but Elara instinctively pulled away, her heart pounding in her chest. The last thing she wanted was to give in to the pull he had on her, to let him drag her back into the chaos of his obsession. She had spent too long living in the shadow of her family's expectations, and now, she couldn't let herself be consumed by his.

"Elara," Julian said, his voice trembling. "Please. I don't want to lose you."

For a moment, Elara felt the familiar ache of longing in her chest, the pull of the love they had shared. But she couldn't allow herself to be dragged back into the storm that had torn them apart. She couldn't lose herself in his madness, his obsession with the rift, the other side, and whatever twisted reality he had created in his mind.

"I can't do this anymore, Julian," Elara said, her voice cracking as she finally spoke the truth that had been building in her for so long. "I can't keep living in this fractured world. I can't keep waiting for you to choose me. I need to move on. I need to be free."

The words hung in the air between them, a final, irreversible decision. She could see the shock on his face, the hurt that flashed in his eyes, but Elara didn't waver. She had given him everything she had, had trusted him, had loved him with everything she was. But she couldn't keep fighting for something that wasn't real anymore.

"I'll never be free until I finish this," Julian said, his voice hollow. "You don't understand, Elara. The rift isn't just a theory. It's the key to everything. It's the only way to understand the world, to understand time, to understand us."

The words stung, and Elara felt the weight of them pressing against her chest. But she couldn't let herself be consumed by them. She had to let go.

"Then go," she said, her voice steady despite the ache in her heart. "Go and find your answers, Julian. But I won't be part of this. I won't let you drag me down with you."

For a long moment, Julian didn't speak. His eyes searched hers, as though he were trying to find something—anything—that would make her change her mind. But Elara stood firm, her heart breaking with every second that passed.

Finally, Julian stepped back, his face shadowed with sorrow. "I'll never forget you, Elara," he whispered. "I'll never forget what we had."

And then, without another word, he turned and walked toward the telescope, his figure a silhouette against the darkening sky. Elara stood there, her breath shaky as she watched him go. The silence that filled the room was deafening. She had let him go. She had made the hardest decision of her life.

But she knew it was the right one. She had to move on. She had to let him fall through his own rift. She couldn't follow him. Not when the man she had once loved was no longer the man she had known.

The air in the observatory felt cold now, empty. Elara walked to the door, her hand trembling as she reached for the handle. She had made her choice. It was time to leave this broken place behind, to step into a new life—one that didn't revolve around Julian's obsession, one that didn't depend on a love that had already started to unravel.

She stepped outside, the cool night air washing over her as she walked away from the observatory, from Julian, from everything that had once held her captive. The city stretched out before her, vast and unfamiliar. But for the first time in a long time, Elara felt free.

And as the rain began to fall again, she knew that this was the only way forward—away from the rift, away from the past, into a future that was hers to create.

www.ingramcontent.com/pod-product-compliance
Lightning Source LLC
LaVergne TN
LVHW010551070526
838199LV00063BA/4943